D1560301

About the Book

Coman Allgood's Book of Inspiration, Empowerment, and Healing is a comprehensive collection of original and famous quotes, sayings, phrases, bible passages, and anecdotes that have had a profoundly positive, uplifting, and motivational effect on Coman throughout his life's personal journey. Coman's father, family, and friends used powerful, impactful words, and quotes that have given him strength. At times this may have meant dealing with the loss of love ones or navigating through challenges in his professional career. He found strength and motivation in the emotional and intellectual power of their words, as they became the light in his darkness, the strength in his weakness, the calm during his anxieties, the courage to make him a warrior in his battle with cancer. These words have inspired him in the accomplishment

2

of one of his proudest moments – completing a full marathon. After spending a lifetime of accumulating and benefiting from these inspirations, Coman has now been moved to share them with world in order to empower others to strive for happiness, peace, and success in all aspects of their life.

Positive Words Give Power to the Soul. One relevant quote on any given day can save a life. Coman's wish is that you read a quote from this book that gives you power in whatever day that you are in. He is thankful to you for you trusting him enough to engage your consciousness with his quotes and inspiration. This book would not exist without the power of the Almighty God.

Amen

About the Author

Coman Allgood is the President of Do Happy Today LLC, which is a positive, inspirational company, providing motivational speaking, t-shirts, and other merchandise. He is the "Happy Coach," a Certified Life Coach, and a Professional International Motivational Speaker and Therapeutic Listening/Advice Coach. For over ten years, he has specialized in coaching and simply listening to individuals and groups all over the world. The listening sessions are the most rewarding part of his business. People want to talk and be heard. As a Psychology graduate of Regent University, he has learned there is nothing more valuable than being heard! Coman is a member of Psi Chi, the International Honor Society in Psychology.

Coman's passion is to help and develop people which has led him to a career in being an international motivational speaker in the US, Canada, Paris, and other parts around the world. Coman Allgood is a mentor, basketball coach, therapeutic listening and advice coach. Coman was also an inspirational speaker for Emory Winship Cancer Institute's Annual 5K race, in support of its fundraising initiatives. He is a frequent guest speaker at churches and other civic events.

Coman Allgood is a native of Atlanta where he grew up. Coman attended Morris Brown College, studying Political Science, and graduated from Regent University, earning a degree in Psychology. Coman has had a great professional career in insurance, mortgages, and business management. He was also a facilitator, supervisor/acting Manager with the USPS. Coman has acted in movies, with his most memorable role being in All Eyez on Me, the Tupac Shakur life story.

Coman is married to his wife Kathie and is the father of Rodney, Zachary, and Maddison.

Disclaimer: A serious effort was made to seek permission and locate the sources of information and quotes when required.

Unintended errors or the inability to locate copyright holders are deeply regretted.

Stay Strong!

"When life gives you lemons, make orange juice and leave the world wondering how you did it"

Section 1

Inspiration

(Positive Affirmations)

You will find the word
"us" in trust; teamwork.

Negative energy;
Ain't nobody got time for
that!

You can't treat a dog like
a puppy.

Your minutes are your lifetime.

Learn to have a memory of a goldfish.

Believing in yourself is more powerful than money.

There's a beginning and a middle; then you decide the ending.

If it makes sense to you, the rest don't matter.

FHL
Forgive, heal and live ...

Be grateful: let that sink in.

You can start again as many times as you like.

The person in the mirror knows you.

Know that, in time, all will be well!

Why worry - The sun is going to come up tomorrow… and go down again.

The past has no legs!

Let go or be dragged.

Always and never…
Always and never apply to
nothing.

Change is acceptance.

Whatever it is you're looking for, will be found.

If you want it bad enough, you will have it!

A good sense of humor is beautiful.

Make smiling your best habit.

That is a serious thang!

What you resist will continue to exist

A successful year of business:
- Mind your own business for 6 months
- Stay out of everybody's else business for 6 months

Silence says a lot...

Success starts with the second letter in the word. U.

You're worth way more than that!

The pain of discipline or the pain of regret.

Hold the vision…

Imagination is the
beginning…

It's easy to be happy when
you're living with happy
people.

There's somebody for
everybody…

Keep it positive: Don't say "KILL two birds with one stone."
Say: "FEED two birds out of one bowl."

Marriage and relationships -It is possible to outgrow each other. It's ok.

Sometimes rock bottom is the best starting place!

A man doesn't just land on top of the mountain.

If you have to keep telling someone something over and over again, you're the one not getting it.

You will get old.

Keep living; it will start making sense!

As a person thinketh, so they are!

Your thoughts are why you are where you are.

Obstacles are what you
see when you take your
eye off your goal.

Get ready to fly:
"What the caterpillar calls
the end of the world, the
master calls a butterfly."
—*Richard Bach*

"The pain I feel now is the happiness I had before. That's the deal."
— *C.S. Lewis*

"There is no pain so great as the memory of joy in present grief."
— *Aeschylus*

"What we have once enjoyed we can never lose. All that we love deeply becomes a part of us."

—*Helen Keller*

"Not everything that is faced can be changed. But nothing can be changed until it is faced,"

—*James Baldwin*

"We are all self-made, but only the successful will admit it."
—*Earl Nightingale*

The thing to do was to act just like others acted, live like they lived, and while they were not looking, do what you wanted.
—*Richard Wright*

"You define your own life. Don't let other people write your script."
—*Oprah Winfrey*

"Believe you can and you're halfway there."
—*Theodore Roosevelt*

"In a gentle way, you can shake the world."
—*Mahatma Gandhi*

"All you need is the plan, the road map, and the courage to press on to your destination."
—*Earl Nightingale*

"Wake up determined; go to bed satisfied."
—*Dwayne "The Rock" Johnson*

"Although the world is full of suffering, it is also full of overcoming it."
—*Helen Keller*

"The most dangerous creation of any society is the man who has nothing to lose."
—*James Baldwin*

"Nobody built like you,
you design yourself."
— *Jay-Z*

"If you don't like the road
you're walking, start
paving another one!"
— *Dolly Parton*

"You are never too old to set another goal or to dream a new dream."
— *C.S. Lewis*

"I believe that if you'll just stand up and go, life will open up for you. Something just motivates you to keep moving."
—*Tina Turner*

"You have to be where you are to get where you need to go."
—*Amy Poehler*

"You must find the place inside yourself where nothing is impossible."
—*Deepak Chopra*

"Whatever you think the world is withholding from you, you are withholding from the world."
—*Eckhart Tolle*

"Courage starts with showing up and letting ourselves be seen."
—*Brené Brown*

"The secret to happiness is freedom … and the secret to freedom is courage."
—*Thucydides*

"You will never do anything in this world without courage. It is the greatest quality of the mind next to honor."
—*Aristotle*

"One man with courage is a majority."
                    —*Thomas Jefferson*

"Failure is unimportant. It takes courage to make a fool of yourself."
                    —*Charlie Chaplin*

"From caring comes courage."

—*Lao Tzu*

"God himself favors the brave."

—*Ovid*

"I'm not funny. What I am is brave."

—*Lucille Ball*

"Our sorrows and wounds are healed only when we touch them with compassion."
— *Buddha*

"As soon as healing takes place, go out and heal somebody else."
— *Maya Angelou*

"You yourself, as much as anybody in the entire universe, deserve your love and affection."
        – *Buddha*

Just try new things. Don't be afraid. Step out of your comfort zones and soar, all right?
        —*Michelle Obama*

A change is brought about
because ordinary people
do extraordinary things.
—*President Barack Obama*

The way to get started is
to quit talking and begin
doing.
—*Walt Disney*

Life is what happens when you're busy making other plans.

— *John Lennon*

"Tell me and I forget.
Teach me and I remember.
Involve me and I learn."

— *Benjamin Franklin*

"Whoever is happy will make others happy too."
—*Anne Frank*

Never let the fear of striking out keep you from playing the game.
—*Babe Ruth*

You will face many
defeats in life, but never
let yourself be defeated.
—*Maya Angelou*

"The only impossible
journey is the one you
never begin."
—*Tony Robbins*

"In this life we cannot do great things. We can only do small things with great love."

—*Mother Teresa*

You can't let your failures define you. You have to let your failures teach you.

—*President Barack Obama*

"Only a life lived for others
is a life worthwhile."
—Albert Einstein

"The purpose of our lives
is to be happy."
—Dalai Lama

"You only live once, but if you do it right, once is enough."

—*Mae West*

"You have brains in your head. You have feet in your shoes. You can steer yourself any direction you choose."

—*Dr. Seuss*

"Life is trying things to see if they work."

—*Ray Bradbury*

"Many of life's failures are people who did not realize how close they were to success when they gave up."

—*Thomas A. Edison*

The secret of success is to
do the common thing
uncommonly well.
—*John D. Rockefeller Jr.*

"There are no secrets to
success. It is the result of
preparation, hard work,
and learning from failure."
—*Colin Powell*

"If you are not willing to risk the usual, you will have to settle for the ordinary."

—*Jim Rohn*

"Winning isn't everything, but wanting to win is."

—*Vince Lombardi*

"Whether you think you can or you think you can't, you're right."

—Henry Ford

"You miss 100% of the shots you don't take."

—Wayne Gretzky

"You become what you believe."

—*Oprah Winfrey*

"Everything you've ever wanted is on the other side of fear."

—*George Addair*

"Too many of us are not living our dreams because we are living our fears."

—*Les Brown*

"I have learned over the years that when one's mind is made up, this diminishes fear."

—*Rosa Parks*

"Do not feel lonely, the entire universe is inside of you."

—*Rumi*

"The universe is under no obligation to make sense to you."

—*Neil DeGrasse Tyson*

Just to be mentioned in the same breath as some of the past winners is amazing. We think this is just real significant.
—*Lanze Thompson*

"Shine like the whole universe is yours."
— *Rumi*

Being great starts with
being grateful.

Time is the most important
thing the world.

When you kill time,
remember that it has no
resurrection.

—*A.W. Tozer*

Patience is delayed gratification.

Pay attention! You'll either pay now or you'll pay later.

A smile has countless meanings!

Eventually, you will see what you think about the most.

Money can only buy so much!

Not everyone is out to get you.

Don't volunteer for the starring role as a victim.

Good positive words from good positive people will make a good positive person.

Say this when you open
your eyes every morning,
"I'm happy to be here."

Make people smile. When
they ask, "How are you?"
Answer, "I'm outstanding
and getting better by the
minute!"

If I look like a fool to you,
you need better glasses.

True love doesn't stop at
color, financial status, or
LGBTQ. I love my
daughter. ♥

I didn't get to pick the color or the type of person for my blood transfusion.

"We can't solve problems by using the same kind of thinking we used when we created them."
—*Albert Einstein*

"When you pray for rain, you gotta deal with the mud too. That's a part of it."

–Denzel Washington

There are 24 hours in a day. That's a lot of time to be happy!

A coach is a counselor, psychologist, teacher, mother, father and a leader. They are also a human being!

Luck is where opportunity meets preparation.

– Denzel Washington

Cancer free -- Amen!

When people stop listening and begin to change, they are on their way back from where they came.

Imagination is the preview of life's coming attractions.

—*Albert Einstein*

Bad attitudes get you to bad places.

The world is changing: are you?

It is all about you, (when) it's all about you!

Once a woman or a man,
twice a child!

–My Dad

Sometimes the wrong
thing to do is the right
thing to do.

One day at a time adds up
to a lifetime!

There's a season for everything!

It's all mental …. all of it.

Grace makes you faithful!

"Laughter is timeless,
imagination has no age,
and dreams are forever."

-Walt Disney

Ignorance is a cure for
nothing.

-W. E. B. Dubois

Love, not blood, makes you family!

Time is all we have.

Success leaves details.

It takes great soil to make a great person!

What they say behind your back will come back to you.

What someone thinks of you is none of your business.

The more you give, the more you receive!

You matter!

Words are powerful.

Pride before fail!

"Seek first to understand,
then to be understood."

-Stephen R. Covey

This no doubt will come
to past.

Life is unpredictable.

Health is more valuable than money.

Love sees no color, only evil does!

If it's built on truth, it will stand.

If it's built on a lie, it won't.

Be faithful to yourself.

You are a great person.

The same wind blows on us all.

I've learned that people will forget what you said, people will forget what you did, but people will never forget how you made them feel.

-Maya Angelou

Nobody cares how much
you know until they know
how much you care.

-Theodore Roosevelt

Out of the mountain of
despair, a stone of hope.

-M. L. King

If you do something often enough, a ratio will appear.

— *Jim Rohn*

Don't complain about a blessing that you prayed for!

-*My Mom*

The best pie is a humble pie!
Stay Humble!

God sees how you treat people when no one else can see.

You have to believe more
in what Jesus can do than
what people can do.

Come here let me give
you a hug
   - *My Mother* ♡

Is that right?
- *My Aunt (When someone is
lying)*

It's the inside of a person that counts not that pretty shell.
- *My Dad*

Understanding is a powerful word.
- *My Dad*

Life is so much better with you in it. Thank you.

Kindness: loaning someone your strength instead of reminding them of their weakness.

When you know what's important, it's easy to ignore what's not.

The greatest luxury is
being free.
> *- Manolo Blahnik*

Sometimes you have to let
go of the picture of what
you thought life would be
and learn to find joy in the
story you're living.

Patience is bitter, but its fruit is sweet.

- *Aristotle*

There is a crack in everything, that's how the light gets in.

-*Leonard Cohen*

The worst thing you can do is to know something and live like you don't. That's robbery.

- *Lisa Nichols*

The universe loves a believer.

No one is you, and that is your power.

- *Dave Grohl*

Your gifts and talents plus
your heart's desire equal
your purpose.

Don't let the fear of what
could happen make
nothing happen.

- *Doe Zantamata*

The sign of a beautiful person is that they always see beauty in others.

Never let anyone— any person or any force— dampen, dim or diminish your light.

- *John Lewis*

Never forget who helped
you out while everyone
else was making excuses.

Remember to take care of
yourself. You can't pour
from an empty cup.

Great spirits have always encountered violent opposition from mediocre minds.

- *Albert Einstein*

I stopped explaining myself when I realized people only understand from their level of perception.

One cannot be prepared
for something while
secretly believing it will
never happen.

- *Nelson Mandela*

Live for the moments you
can't put into words.

Bloom with grace.

Let go of negativity, focus on the good.

Sometimes you must forget what you feel and remember what you deserve.

See with your ears and hear with your eyes.

- *Ken Kesey*

It takes 17 muscles in your face to smile, but it takes 43 muscles to frown.

Aging is just another word for living.

Life is better when you're laughing.

When words are both true
and kind, they can change
the world.

- *Buddha*

Those who think they
know it all have no way of
finding out they don't.

- *Leo Buscaglia*

Don't let yourself be controlled by three things: people, money, or past experiences.

No one else is supposed to understand your calling, it wasn't a conference call.

No drama zone. Don't
bring that mess around
here.

Lost time is never found
again.

- *Benjamin Franklin*

You can't tell big dreams
to small minded people.

- *Steve Harvey*

Don't let someone who has
done nothing tell you how
to do anything.

If you cannot be positive,
then at least be quiet.

- *Joel Osteen*

Section 2

Empowerment

(You Can Do It!)

When the best is possible, good is not an option.

He who angers you, owns you.

Celebrate, celebrate and celebrate; you are worth it!

There are 3 ways of
learning:
Seeing,
Doing,
Listening.

Stay focused; focus on
staying focused.

Say this slowly three
times:
I am free…
I am free…
I am free!

Repetition is the definition
of winning!

It hurts, but the lesson is more important.

Be positive, think positive....

Do Happy Today!

Love yourself.

PCO- Positive
Conversation Only!

Fasting is good.

You know better than that.
-Grandma

The more you bend, the
more you show your ass!
-Tony Ciotti (my father-in-law)

Be drama free.

Your thoughts create your life.

Don't be afraid to use your gift!

If it's important enough to you, you will do it.

You had a dream, now do something!

You have to do something.

-My Dad

You are the deal maker in every situation.

Positive self-talk is the best self-talk.

Rule number one in life: Respect Time!

Think about the what if, before you do it.

Quitting is not an option;
making adjustments is.
Never give up!

Your job is not a death
sentence.
You are free to leave at
any time!

It may not be easy, but it's
worth it!

It's how you handle what happens to you that matters! I am a Cancer survivor.

-Coman K. Allgood

Habits create dreams.

You have nothing to lose. Go for it!

Pray, eat healthy, sleep, exercise.
We only have one body!

Breathe, breathe and breathe.

Let people be. It's not your business.

Only give when asked: advice.

If Jesus can wash someone's feet you can volunteer! Serve!

Be happy for someone else when it's their light in the sun. ☀

Don't stop until you find some way to help someone.

A positive mind is all you need!

Your will, will take you places.

If a man/woman can go to the moon you can achieve your goal.

Travel alone if no one wants to go!

Yes, one woman or man can have all that power…. You.

Stressed spelled backwards is desserts. Controlling your emotions brings sweet experiences.

Stop 2nd guessing yourself.

To be a champion you
have to hang around
champions.

Keep smart people around
you.

Keep doing what works.
Stop doing what doesn't
working.

Walk away; just walk away.

If you want something different, you have to have a different way of thinking.

Losing hurts.

Winning feels great!

Celebrate your yourself!

Instead of finding things
in people to "X" them out,
find things in people to
accept them in.

When people throw
stones, throw seeds back,
so they can grow.

Love yourself.

Rebuke the devil in the
name of Jesus.

Stop drinking, smoking and doping. Your old age will thank you in advance.

It is as easy as you make it.

When people say, "Leave me alone," leave them alone.

Don't you dare go back after the way that you were treated!

An apple a day keeps the doctor away!

It's ok to be scared, nervous, and afraid. But remember the other team is not!

Stay away from fools.
You'll only hurt yourself
trying to help them.

Some people learn by
seeing!

Every successful person
was a student of a
successful person.

You may have to watch him/her crash and burn. Life's a teacher.

Help those that want to be helped.

What's in you must come out!

You deserve to be happy in your life.

Treat your pet like you want to be treated!

Are you trying to be someone else? Breaking news: you will never get it right.

You may have to talk their language to be understood!

Seek to understand first.

You can change the past today!

You cannot be in a relationship with a person that refuses / will not listen.

You learn more with your mouth shut.

Ok turns into good;

Good turns into great;

Great turns into
excellence;

Excellence turns into
legendary.

Your brain is powerful.

Nothing beats a try!

Do things for the right reason.

If you can help someone, help someone.

You're ok! Nobody's perfect!

How many days have you made it through tough times? All of them.

No risk no reward. Take a chance!

You'll find the right one
when you hold yourself to
a higher standard.

If you sow seeds of beans,
don't be surprised when
beans show up.

In due season your harvest
will come.

Your parents didn't raise no fool-

Get it together!

It's not what you get; it's what you become after you get it.

Keep doing what works!

Work hard on developing yourself; you are the beginning to your life.

If a tree is not producing fruit, you must cut it down.

People only take you seriously when you're serious.

Celebrate yourself!
Nobody has to know
what's going on.

All our dreams can come
true, if we have the
courage to pursue them.

- Walt Disney

Persistency *and*
consistency wins
championships!

Say this every day: I will never be broke again!

-*Les Brown*

Just at least try.

One of the keys to success is knowing what and who to ignore.

You have to let other people help you.

Just go take a walk.

There are no bad days. There are only character-building days!

Focus on a positive
outcome!

There's no time for
stupidity.

Worrying changes
nothing; only action does.

If you tried it and it didn't work, try again another way.

You will think about it, but don't quit!

Forgive but don't be a fool.

If a person won't listen,
stop talking.

If you listen, you can hear.

Do what you do best;
leave the rest up to
someone else.

Earn your place; you will value it more.

All money ain't good money!

-My Dad

All candy ain't sweet.

-My Dad

BOOK OF INSPIRATION, EMPOWERMENT & HEALING

Everything that glitters
don't shine.

-My Dad

There's nothing that you
can do with an idiot.

-My Dad

Yes, we can!

Sometimes you win and
sometimes you learn.

It's good to have friends
of all walks of life.

Never give up!

You can learn from everyone; they'll teach you what to do and what not to do.

Be good to yourself!

-President Barack Obama

Love wins over hate!

Nobody gets out alive, so have fun while you're here.

Speak words of encouragement.

Don't let your past use too much of your future.

It's not the size of the dog in the fight; it's the size of the fight in the dog that's in the fight!

Respect the dog for the owner.

-Tony Ciotti (my father-in-law)

Keep your house clean
and it will feel like you
live in a mansion.

-Shirley Ciotti (my mother-in-law)

You get one ride on the
carousel of life; have fun.

Most importantly, if you've done all that you can do, then it's All Good.

When everything is said and done there is nothing left to do or say.

-- *Darryl Dawkins*

Be an instrument of peace!

All that you have been through has brought you here.

What you don't know *will* hurt you.

Make yourself proud of yourself!

The dirt is necessary.
A flower doesn't grow without pushing through the dirt.

-Steve Harvey

You have to do something to get something.

You may have to wean
your way off of your bad
habits a little at a time and
work your way toward
your good habits a little at
a time.
You're not a cold Turkey!

There's a genius born
every minute of the day.

Know the difference
between sugar and salt,
before you taste it!

Be positive!
Rain is liquid sunshine ☼

You are here to do great
things.

Don't let money change
you.

Never look down or talk
negative behind people's
backs. It's a reflection of
who you are.

If they do it with you, they will do it to you! (Let that sink in)

- Kathie Allgood

Relationships!
Go slow. Sugar water turns into shit water quick.

- My Dad ♡

What's real:
If you look at it long
enough you'll see!
- *My Dad*

You never know what's
going on behind the doors
of someone else's big
pretty house. Take care of
what's in your house.
- *My Dad*

Buy a car that's going to last a long time. That other stuff don't matter.
- *My Dad*

Sometimes people respect you more when they think that you're dumb.
- *My Dad* 🏆

The boiling water that softens the potato also hardens the egg. It's not about the elements, rather it's what you are made of.

Forgive yourself for not knowing what you didn't know before you learned it.

Never complain about what your parents couldn't give you. It was probably all they had.

You cannot reach your goals of the future if you have one foot still chained to the failures of your past.

Success isn't about how much money you make; it's about the difference you make in people's lives.

- *Michelle Obama*

Go after your dream, no matter how unattainable others think it is.

Listen and silent are spelled with the same letters. Think about it.

Be careful how you talk to yourself because You are listening.

How long should you try?
Until you make it happen.

Falling down is an
accident; staying down is
a choice.

One mistake does not have
to control your whole life.

The more you celebrate
your life, the more there is
in life to celebrate.
- *Oprah Winfrey*

When was the last time
you did something for the
first time?

Never put the key to your happiness in someone else's pocket.

The moment you realize how important time is, your entire perspective will change.

- *Unknown*

You don't know this new me; I put back my pieces, differently.
- *High Poets Society*

Take care of your body. It's the only place you have to live in.

Rest when you need to,
but never quit.
- *John Wooden*

Nothing can dim the light
that shines from within.
- *Maya Angelou*

I had to make you
uncomfortable, otherwise
you never would have
moved.
- *Universe*

A positive mind finds
opportunity in everyone.

People will never forget
how you made them feel.
- *Maya Angelou*

Don't just be eye candy, be soul food.

Don't let someone else's opinion of you become your reality.
- *Les Brown*

Give yourself time.

No matter how educated, talented, rich, or cool you believe you are, how you treat people ultimately tells all.

Never let your emotions overpower your intelligence.

The past is in your head.
The future is in your
hands.

It's time to focus on what
matters.

We can become so fixated
on achieving success that
we do not pay attention to
what really counts.
- *Garth Jestley*

Sometimes in life, your situation will keep repeating itself until you learn your lesson.

Hey warrior keep going!

There are far better things ahead than any we leave behind.

- *C.S. Lewis*

Stand up and finish what you started.

- *Bob Harper*

I don't fix problems. I fix my thinking. Then problems fix themselves.

First they ignore you, then they laugh at you, then they fight you, then you win.

- *Gandhi*

I'm not telling you it is going to be easy, I'm telling you it's going to be worth it.

Be sure to taste your words before you spit them out.

I only want to be around positive motivational energy.

No more distractions, it's time to be selfish.

You're a fighter. Look at everything you've overcome. Don't give up now.

-   *Olivia Benson*

I may not be there yet, but I'm closer than I was yesterday.

If you think the way you used to think, you'll do the things you used to do.

- *Andy Stanley*

Hey dreamer, keep dreaming. Hey warrior, keep going.

- *Saloni Jain*

Don't wish, do.

You are free to make whatever choice you want, but you are not free from the consequences of the choice.

You can't fail if you never quit.

Don't listen to what they say. Go see.

Persistence -- the ability to keep moving forward, in spite of difficulties.

- *Byron Pulsifer*

Don't just sit there. Do something. The answers will follow.

- *Mark Manson*

Consistency is what transforms average into excellence.

No matter who you are, no matter what you did, no matter where you've come from, you can always change and become a better version.

The key to success is to start before you are ready.

- *Marie Forleo*

Leadership is based on inspiration, not domination; on cooperation, not intimidation.

- *William Arthur wood*

Follow your dreams. Or you'll spend the rest of your life working for someone who did.

All we have to decide is what to do with the time that is given us.

- *J.R.R. Tolkien*

What you do today is important because you are exchanging a day of your life for it.

- *Unknown*

Nobody looks better than when they are helping someone else.

- *Kevin Kling*

Until it is my turn, I will happily applaud others.

I have been fighting since I was a child. I am not a survivor, I am a warrior.

Ask for what you want
and be prepared to get it.

- *Maya Angelou*

Y'all are making your kids
soft. When I was five I
died once and mom made
me walk it off…

Your habits decide your
future --act accordingly.

Karma has no deadline.

Never let the things you
want make you forget the
things you have.

Stop imagining fake
scenarios and hurting your
own feelings.

When you want to succeed
as bad as you want to
breathe, then you will be
successful.

- *Eric Thomas*

Surround yourself with positive people who are going to push you toward greatness.

You cannot hang out with negative people and expect to live a positive life.

I have a mustard seed, and I'm not afraid to use it!

Your perception is your reality.

GBG: go be great!

Everything that exists in your life, does so because of two things: something you did or something you didn't do.

- *Albert Einstein*

Appreciate what you have, before it turns into what you had.

Don't judge people by their past, they don't live there anymore.

Don't get sidetracked by people who are not on track.

Starve your distractions, feed your focus.

Don't let the tamed ones
tell you how to live.

- *Jonny Ox*

When the why is clear, the
how is easy.

I changed my thinking. It changed my life.

- *Unknown*

Start where you are. Use what you have. Do what you can.

- *Arthur Ashe*

Some of the best advice
I've been given: don't take
criticism from someone
you wouldn't take advice
from.

- *Morgan Freeman*

If you never try you'll
never know.

Before you speak…
THINK

T - is it true?

H - is it helpful?

I - is it inspiring?

N - is it necessary?

K - is it kind?

Section 3

Healing
(Spiritual Power)

In a crisis, Christ is there!

Psalms 91

If there's no mother or father: there's always Mother Earth and Father God.

One faithful prayer can change your life.

Genesis 50:20

When you pray, pray an honest prayer.

Trust in God. God will trust you.

Write the vision and make it plain.

- *Habakkuk 2.2 KJV*

God is in control.

Sometimes, it takes a painful experience to make us change our ways.

Just pray about it.

Feeling your body and spirit living is far better than feeling your body dying.

Good people are like candles; they burn themselves up to give others light.

Count it ALL good.

There is power in prayer!

No matter how much it hurts, you have to hold your head up and keep going.

No one will take your joy away from you.

- *John 16:22*

The future is as bright as your faith.

- *Bill Dedman*

The moment you're ready to quit is usually the moment right before a miracle happens.
Don't give up.

Each new day has a different shape to it. You just roll with it.

Dear Past,
Thank you for all the lessons.
Dear Future,
I'm now ready.

Healing does not mean the damage never existed. It means the damage no longer controls our lives.

It costs $0.00 to be grateful for what you already have.

Nobody can take what
God has for you.

The more you pray, the
more protection you have.

Listen to the wisdom of
the toothless one.
          - *Proverb*

Let each of you look out
not only for his own
interests, but also for the
interests of others.

- Philippians 2: 4

You can either focus on
what's tearing you apart or
what's holding you
together.

Whatever's good for your soul... do that!

"The only thing worse than being blind is having sight but no vision."
- *Helen Keller*

Jesus is everywhere!

Kindness is the language
which the deaf can hear
and the blind can see.

What is yours will find
you.

A perfect day is when the
soul smiles.

The greatest gift you can receive, is another day of life.

You're gonna make it after all.

Our words enlarge or restrict our potential.

Those who leave
everything in God's hand,
will eventually see God's
hand and everything.

- *Amen*

Hope is the little voice
you hear whisper "maybe"
when it seems the entire
world is shouting "no!"

Sometimes you have to lose your mind to find your freedom.

Make peace with your broken pieces.

If you're going through hell keep going.

- *Winston Churchill*

Stay positive even when it feels like your life is falling apart.

When you least expect it, God answers and miracles happen.

To heal a wound you need to stop touching it.

And the day came when the risk to remain tight in a bud was more painful than the risk it took to blossom.

- *Anais Nin*

Strength grows in the moments when you think you can't go on but you keep going anyway.

When 'I' is replaced with 'We', even illness becomes Wellness.

- *Malcolm X*

To really be free, you need to be free in the mind.

- *Alexander Loutsis*

Remember that big thing you were afraid of? You survived that. You'll survive again.

Do not stand in a place of danger trusting in miracles.

-   *African Proverb*

Someone else is praying for the things you take for granted.

Let the one among you
who is without sin be the
first to cast a stone.

- *Jesus*

When the prayer becomes
your habit, miracles
become your lifestyle.

No matter how long it takes, when God works, it's always worth the wait.

The only way God can show us he's in control is to put us in situations we can't control.

- *Steven Furtick*

The best way to pay for a lovely moment is to enjoy it.

- *Richard Bach*

Love yourself fully, deeply, honestly, faithfully, gloriously.

Another day is a blessing.
Don't take it for granted.

A healthy attitude is
contagious but don't wait
to catch it from others. Be
a carrier.

- *Tom Stoppard*

Faith it till you make it.

Only God can turn a mess
into a message, a test into
a testimony, a trial into a
triumph, a victim into a
victory.

- *Unknown*

Keep your face towards
the sunshine and shadows
will fall behind you.

- *Walt Whitman*

The one who angers you
controls you.

- *Tracy James*

Being happy never goes
out of style.

- *Lily Pulitzer*

In anger we should refrain both from speech and action.

- *Pythagoras*

Strength: a river cuts through a rock not because of its power but its persistence.

Do the best you can until you know better. Then when you know better, do better.

- *Maya Angelou*

Trials without God will break you, but trials with God will make you.

Life is a one-time offer, use it well.

Don't let anyone change who you are, to become what they need.

Your story is the key that
can unlock someone else's
prison. Share your
testimony.

- *Spiritual inspiration*

Never forget who was
there for you when no one
else was.

Choose to be optimistic, it feels better.

- *Dalai Lama*

Soon, when all is well, you're going to look back on this period of your life and be glad that you never gave up.

If you are waking up with the sensation that there has got to be more in life…
Then there is.

- *Steve Harvey*

You cannot treat people like garbage and worship God at the same time.

We are going to love you no matter what, We don't care what you do or where you go, and don't you ever forget that.

- My mom and Dad would say this to me in my darkest moments in my life.

If you have read these
quotes to this point:
God loves you!

Email me at;
allgoodvoice@gmail.com
for your free gift.

Thank you.